Wicca

A Beginner's Guide to Wiccan Witchcraft

Cassandra Miller

Table of Contents

An Ancient Faith 1

Chapter 1: Polytheism and Nature 8

Chapter 2: The Wiccan Rede 15

Chapter 3: Wheel of The Year 19

Chapter 4: Altars 23

Chapter 5: Working Tools 28

Chapter 6: Putting It Together 35

Chapter 7: Spells and Rituals 43

Conclusion 53

A Self-Initiation 55

An Ancient Faith

The religion of Wicca has been around far longer than many people realize and has changed with the times. It is not simply a group of dark-robed people standing around a cauldron concocting curses, but instead a serious faith with a rich history. It has touched every country in the world in some way, whether through historical influence or modern practitioners choosing to honor ancient deities. But despite this extensive history and influence, this faith is still heavily tied up in negative imagery that impacts the willingness people have to learn more about it.

When a person hears the word Wicca, their thoughts inevitably go to some predictable stereotypes. Very few people seem to be aware that Wicca and its practices predate many modern religions and even some ancient ones. This is a faith founded on respect for nature, respect for the self, and the idea of balance in all things. Many Wiccans blend different religious faiths or aspects of different cultures into their personal religious practice; in fact, much of Wicca is a flexible faith. There are only a few shared tenets among practitioners.

Wicca has no formally recognized churches or temples. Most practitioners work alone or in small groups commonly known as covens. Some attend non-denominational churches that are accepting of all faiths, such as the Unitarian Universalist church.

Wicca as a whole is surrounded by stereotypes and mystery. Its symbols are unique and can represent many different faiths and cultures, and its practitioners live all over the world. Some are open about their practice, and some are not, but all are devout to the deities or ideals they choose to uphold.

Many Wiccans are not open about their faith for fear of being judged based on misconceptions. Wiccans have been punished for their faith throughout history in many different countries; despite this, it's not uncommon for Wiccan practices to become adopted into modern society. These practices have been so thoroughly claimed by people outside of the Wiccan faith that their origins have been almost entirely forgotten. One goal of this book is to educate readers and explain the truth about this ancient belief system that has captivated many in the modern era; the other is to introduce people to this different system of faith that is welcoming to all.

Wicca: No More Misconceptions

Most Wiccans do not worship Satan. In fact, most Wiccans do not believe in any single entity who embodies all evil. Likewise, they do not believe in Hell or any similar place of eternal torment or judgement. Satan and Hell belong solely to the Christian faith and have no role in Wicca. Some Wiccans choose to worship deities from other cultures, such as cultures shared by their family or homeland. Some choose to pray to their ancestors, relying on the wisdom of those who came before. Others might pray to a nameless god or goddess. Still others prefer to simply honor and respect nature without referencing a specific deity or considering any greater power than their own will.

Many Wiccans believe in an afterlife in the form of Summerland. This is believed to be a place where nature is continually blooming and growing; everything is fertile and green, and all weariness and illness is gone. Family members are reunited in this beautiful land. This afterlife is a paradise for nature-worshipping Wiccans.

The spellwork performed in Wicca is specified as *magick* as opposed to magic. This is a simple spelling commonality that is intended to separate Wiccan spells and prayers from card tricks or sleight of hand. The two should not be conflated; where one is a series of deeply rooted cultural practices, the other is merely entertainment. Wicca is a religion that involves neither tricks nor luck nor much of the supernatural (though some do consider the supernatural an important part of their practice, as we will continue to discuss).

Some Wiccans may choose to use Ouija boards or other methods to communicate with the dead, but this rarely looks like a shadowy seance ending with the lights flickering on and off and someone getting possessed. Those who choose to deal with such forces do so with caution and respect. They would no sooner order the dead around than they would tell a god or goddess what to do. Rather, Wiccans who choose to make contact with spirits or ghosts will usually do so to try and learn from them. They might want to learn more about themselves, the spirits in question, or why they linger. This practice is very individualized from one Wiccan to another; some behave as ghost hunters, seeking them out to learn about their lives and to send them peacefully away. Others just pray to their ancestors for guidance.

Modern Wiccans do not perform animal sacrifices or deliberately hurt other people. Killing animals isn't a common practice for anyone who reveres nature; while it may have been more commonplace in the past, it is now considered taboo. That being said, do not stereotype all Wiccans as goofy, tree-hugging pacifists; vegetarianism, veganism, and pacifism are not required of Wiccans. While most Wiccans avoid harming others through their own actions, they know that conflict is unavoidable in life and that there are times it cannot be prevented. They usually try to send out positive energy and hope for the best outcome in any situation. A common saying in Wicca is that the more magick you know, the less you use it. This is because Wiccans tend to use spells as a last resort. They will always try to find mundane solutions to their problems first.

Let's address another common stereotype. Sex magick exists in Wicca, but it is only practiced between consenting adults and is never a public act in any way. Practicing in the nude (called "going skyclad") is likewise only done in private and with advanced warning to other coven members. Not every Wiccan is part of a coven, and they do not have to be. Likewise, Wicca is open for anyone who wishes to learn. There is no formalized learning a person must have to call themselves a Wiccan and no requirement to have a Wiccan in your family in order to practice. This is not a faith tied to heredity or specific honors or labels; anyone with the desire to learn is free to do their own research and join this diverse and eclectic system of faith in whatever way they choose.

The only difference here involves covens, in which rules about formalized learning can change. Some covens have approved training that they pass on to initiates in order to keep a base level of shared knowledge within the group. The knowledge held by covens can sometimes come in levels depending on a person's amount of involvement within the group. A common knowledge base usually consists of the deities the coven prays to, their personal traditions and established guardians, and other basics. In addition to providing newcomers with mentors and teachers, covens provide a central system of support and community revolving around a common set of practices (for example, where every coven member prays to the same deity).

Origins Of Wicca

Many Wiccan practices were born out of parts of many different religious faiths. Throughout history, cultures have conquered and colonized each other, claiming land and people as they went. When it came to attempts to teach or spread their faith, the conquering nation was sometimes careful to spread its own religion in a manner that would not entirely alienate the natives in the hopes of getting it to stick. To encourage this, they would sometimes tweak native religious practices to fit their own faiths. An example of this is the Christmas tree, which started as an ancient pagan practice; pagans would bring green branches into their homes in the winter as a way to remind themselves that the cold would not last forever, and spring would still return. Christians blended that tradition with their own Christmas celebrations in an attempt to bring pagans over to their faith, and the Christmas tree eventually became so popular that its origins were forgotten.

This is far from the only borrowed practice that came from Wicca. It is also not the sole example of faiths merging throughout history. This common practice has led to modern Wicca merging with ancient faiths, which is a historical fascination in itself. The number of pantheons and traditions available to modern Wiccans is dizzying; likewise, the rich history of this faith is fascinating to examine and study.

Anti-witchcraft laws and propaganda are not unusual in history. Even before the famed Salem, Massachusetts witch trials there were plenty of anti-witchcraft attitudes in the United States and many other countries. So many pagan rituals had been absorbed into conquering civilizations that some countries and their faiths had been completely and utterly changed. Animal sacrifices fell out of common practice following the spread of Christianity, and the art of revering nature became less common as more and more churches sprang up and gathered more political power. As other faiths spread and Wicca was forced further into the dark, a change was due. It happened in England, thanks to a man by the name of Gerald Gardner.

Gerald Gardner is responsible for laying down most of the Wiccan practices that exist today. Gardner had studied many faiths from all around the world including Kabbalah, the Jewish tree of life that illustrates how God's creative energies were spread throughout the universe. He was also influenced by the works of Aleister Crowley, who believed in seeking out one's true purpose and pursuing self-knowledge in order to merge with the larger universe. In addition to all of this, Gardner was also strongly influenced by the practices of his own New Forest coven.

All of these sources combined to create the first public knowledge of the Wiccan faith. The Gardnerian Path was introduced in the 1950s with features such as a degree system and a required period of initiation. This systemic approach inspired rumors that a person could only follow Wicca if they had been properly initiated, but this is yet another misconception. Gardnerian Wicca introduced the Book of Shadows, a personal book in which each Wiccan writes down their spells. The original Books of Shadows were written by one member of a coven, and then other members would copy it and add their own knowledge at the end. In this way, every Book of Shadows was sure to be unique to the person who made it while still containing the shared knowledge of the coven.

Gardner brought Wiccan practices to light immediately after many anti-witchcraft laws were repealed in England. He wrote a book, *Witchcraft Today*, which has been updated and reprinted many times throughout the years. Gardnerian practices remain mostly closed due to their initiation practices and degree system, but this is the exception rather than the rule. Privacy within covens does not bar the practice of Wicca from anyone else.

One of Gardner's students by the name of Raymond Buckland brought Wicca to America and helped to spread the word about the new faith. Buckland founded a tradition known as Seax-Wicca that was based on Saxon themes. Unlike Gardnerian tradition, this system had no sense of secrecy to it, and knowledge of Wicca became available to even more people. Buckland is a prolific author and has written many different works discussing the study and practice of the Wiccan faith.

Another important figure in Wiccan history was Scott Cunningham, a student of Buckland's. He wrote and published *Wicca: A Guide For The Solitary Practitioner*. This book served as a nail in the coffin for Gardnerian practices. Wicca could be practiced by any person in the world regardless of their membership to a coven, a formal initiation, or a degree earned through the granting of secret knowledge. It was available to anyone and everyone.

These are far from the only significant figures in Wicca's history. However, they are widely recognized as some of the most important, and their records and works help to explain this religion's recognition and spread. Modern Wicca is accessible to anybody who has an interest in it, though some sects remain more secretive. Those that maintain this more secretive style of faith are following the example set by Gerald Gardner and the New Forest coven he joined. Though a multitude of traditions exist, there is truly no one single way to practice Wicca. This is a faith that welcomes anyone who is willing to put in an effort to try to become a more wholly aware person.

Chapter 1: Polytheism and Nature

There are over one million practitioners of Wicca on the planet. Each one of them is likely to follow the same basic tenets and many of the same customs. They share a faith that encourages its practitioners to take their lives into their own hands. Through the manipulation of energies otherwise known as spell casting, Wiccans can often bring more positivity into their lives and the lives of those around them. These unique practices and beliefs are some of the most interesting and diverse a person can find, especially when it is all grouped under the label of a single faith.

Some modern Wiccans choose to honor the spirits of nature, whether through the various elements or other spirits such as the fae. This may be one of the simplest forms of deity seen in Wicca. In fact, the idea of respecting nature is one of the most commonly held beliefs among Wiccans. The only difference is whether or not those Wiccans also choose to pray to a goddess or a god. Those who do not will usually focus their practice around the idea of living in balance with nature rather than trying to honor or please a given deity.

The most common nature deities in Wicca are Mother Nature and the Green Man. The former is familiar to most people and depicted as a fertile goddess who usually embodies the globe. The Green Man looks like a man of the wild, usually depicted with a beard of moss and hair plaited with oak leaves. Both are straightforward nature deities, meant to symbolize greenery, life, and the cycle of the seasons.

Living in balance with nature (as with most other things Wicca) can look very different for different people. Some people choose to make lifestyle changes to exemplify living mindfully of nature. They might recycle everything, change their diet to vegetarianism or veganism, and encourage others to follow their lead. Other Wiccans may make those changes without broadcasting them to the wider world. Still others will simply cut out meat for meals once a week and take a walk every day. All of these people are honoring nature in the way that works best for them.

Whether honoring nature or a specific deity, most of the practices will look similar to an outside observer. Many Wiccans pray or meditate as a regular practice in their daily life. They leave offerings to either a deity or a nature spirit or both. They will make requests and ask for blessings or good outcomes for struggles in their lives. They show thanks for the blessings they have been given. In all these practices, Wicca looks very similar to most other popular religions. However, one of the largest religious differences comes in the form of Wicca's unique polytheism.

Choosing to worship or honor deities is another step many take in their practice of Wicca. This can be a difficult decision, with some Wiccans choosing to simply pray to a god or goddess without assigning any specific names to those deities. Still others are drawn to very specific deities to pray to.

This can happen for a variety of reasons. Some people choose which deities to pray to based on their own family history, such as a country of origin. Others are drawn to a specific culture whether they have familial ties to it or not. Still others may be called to a specific deity and look into that deity's pantheon as a result. With many ancient pantheons to choose from, it can be a difficult decision; narrowing the choices down to only a pair can be even harder. This can lead to someone praying to specific deities for specific needs rather than settling on just one or two. Some examples include offering prayers of protection to a war deity for a soldier or praying to an agrarian deity to bring abundance into your life.

Reaching out to a specific deity can be symbolic or literal. A person can pray to a goddess of motherhood for a safe pregnancy or to be blessed with the patience of a mother who always has to multi-task. Truly, anything involving deities can grow complicated quickly in Wicca. One common practice to simplify things is to split the deity or deities into individual trifectas, similar to the Christian trinity of Father, Son, and Holy Ghost.

This idea of three in one is not exclusive to Christianity. It can be found in the Greek Fates, the Irish Morrigan, Alilat in Arabian folklore, and many more faiths. This commonality extends even to Wicca. In Wicca, the God and Goddess are divided into three for the roles that each are intended to play in the lives of their worshippers. These roles are thought to reflect the aging process we go through ourselves, and are perhaps a nod to the idea that humanity was created in a deity's image.

The Goddess: Maiden, Mother, Crone

The Goddess plays a very important role in Wicca and is commonly symbolized by the moon. The moon's phases are thought to reflect feminine energy, hence the connection to the Goddess. She is often honored much more than her male counterpart. This might come as a surprise considering the dominant influence male deities have in so many other cultures and religions. Some Wiccans choose to honor and pray only to the Goddess and include the God as an afterthought, if at all.

The Goddess trifecta is divided into maiden, mother, and crone. The maiden embodies youth, bright energy, and boldness. She is the youngest aspect of the Goddess, tied to spring, innocence, creativity, and joy. She is represented by the waxing moon, symbolizing a new beginning full of possibilities. This aspect of the Goddess may be honored by new practitioners or those who are about to start a new phase of life. Some common examples of maiden-aligned goddesses include Artemis, Brigid, or Airmid.

The mother Goddess is more mature, represented by the full moon. She often personifies nature itself, representing the full bounty of the earth. These goddesses are depicted as patient and wise, commonly ruling over domains such as motherhood, fertility, and creation. This aspect is honored by those who are looking for stability or patience, qualities more commonly seen in older women. Some mother goddesses include Isis, Hera, and Asada Ya.

The third aspect is the crone, represented by the waning moon. The crone has age, wisdom, and patience on her side. Those who think she is easily dismissed will be corrected in the proper time; she is just as strong a force as any other Goddess. She is known as a holder of mysteries, offering wisdom and detachment from material desires to those who reach out to her. The crone has nothing left to lose and revels in the resultant freedom from that state. Some crone goddesses include Hecate, Kali, and Baba Yaga.

In some ways, these three aspects reflect views of femininity in both ancient and modern societies. This is slightly sad, as the crone is sometimes forgotten or dismissed in some circles. There are many modern Wiccans, however, who are reclaiming the title of crone and revel in their own wisdom and advanced ages. This revival has helped bring more positive attention to the crone herself, offering more respect to this equally important aspect of the Goddess. The three Goddess aspects work together as part of their three-in-one trinity. Wiccans need not choose only one deity or one aspect to worship; each one has something to teach, things to bless, and aspects of life that they can exercise control over. This is why some Wiccans choose to pray to multiple deities or even the trinity aspect of the Goddess as a whole without applying any names to Her.

The God: Youth, Warrior, Sage

The God as a whole is sometimes forgotten or dismissed outright in Wicca, but just as with the minimization of the role of the crone, this can be a mistake. The God is the Goddess's other half. By representing masculinity, he helps to keep the masculine and feminine energies in balance in the same fashion as earth, air, water, and fire are kept in balance around the four quadrants of a magick circle. The God is depicted as solar energy, more constant and level than the ever-changing phases of the moon. The God is also seen as a hunter with common dominion over wild animals. He is a protector, guardian, and provider. Whatever his chosen name, he too has three stages in his trinity just as the Goddess does.

The youth is fresh-faced and curious; he represents freedom as well as limitations. Though he is strong, he can depend on that physical strength too much and not enough on wisdom. He has great curiosity about the world, but may be reluctant to leave familiar territory. He has not been judged by life yet and still has a positive outlook. He favors self-discovery and may have an academic focus. Examples of youth gods include Apollo, Thor, and Aengus.

The warrior is a provider and decision maker. He is more mature, patient, and a consummate protector. While the mother provides and nurtures, the warrior keeps everyone safe. These gods are more careful, perhaps, but no less powerful than their youthful counterparts. Common warrior deities include Lugh, Hephaestus, and Dagda.

The sage is the third aspect, a savant and mentor to whomever seeks him out. This last stage for the God, much like its crone counterpart, is underestimated by many Wiccans. Sage deities tend to be quite powerful, but very still and stoic. They only act when it suits them, and they behave deliberately. Most would probably prefer to teach patient lessons to their followers rather than demonstrate some massive show of power or ability. Common sage deities include Hades, Ra, and Odin.

Again, each of these aspects work together. Calling on one God over another may be a better choice if someone is looking for specific spellwork or a certain outcome. Nevertheless, honoring multiple deities or at least the multiple aspects of one deity seems a wise idea. This causes many Wiccans to offer prayers to multiple names, though they may only have two specific deities on their altars. Worshipping a goddess without at least recognizing a god or male aspect throws off that all-important sense of balance which is so important to the Wiccan tradition. The circles are cast in quarters; the deities have male and female aspects. Offering recognition to both or none at all seems more natural than offering to just one.

There are alternate options to worshiping any deity or giving offerings to the spirits of nature. Some Wiccans choose to look to their ancestors for wisdom or guidance, praying to deceased family members for whatever supernatural intervention they might need. Another option is to revere specific animals or plants that one might have an affinity toward. This is commonly referred to as a familiar or a spirit animal, and does not need to be a pet or even an animal that is physically in the Wiccan's home or on the planet. Wiccan altars can be dedicated to a deity, an animal, deceased family, or simply set up as a beacon to draw in positive energy and banish negativity. All these methods are equally valid forms of Wiccan deity worship.

Chapter 2: The Wiccan Rede

The word *rede* means counsel or advice. This ancient word has been applied to many declarations and stories over the years; in Wicca, it is used as an explanation of the faith's practices. While other faiths may teach their practice through parables, stories, sermons, or formal teachings, the Wiccan faith has a slightly different approach.

The Wiccan Rede is the title given to a poem that lays out guidelines for how the faith works. It was first publicly published in 1974 and was allegedly being used by covens at least ten years prior to that date. This collection of couplets is widely accepted as an overview of Wiccan beliefs. It describes the cardinal directions and makes mention of which elements are tied to each. Some of the major Wiccan holidays, known collectively as Sabbats, are given mention. The idea of casting spells in rhyme is mentioned, as well as other Wiccan traditions.

Perhaps the most important of these guidelines is summed up in the final couplet:

Eight words the Wiccan Rede fulfill: "if it harm none, do as ye will."

In other words, as long as Wiccans are not harming anyone or anything, they are able to do whatever they desire. Even the message of the Wiccan Rede is not particularly original to the Rede itself. Gerald Gardner made reference to the same rule, borrowing it from a literary creation from 1901. The idea was also mentioned in 1904 by Aleister Crowley; one of the earliest recorded mentions of this rule is in the 1500s, though it may have existed prior to that century.

The twenty-six couplets of the Wiccan Rede were originally credited to Gwen Thompson. She further credits it to her grandmother as the original source. The Rede was published not only to spread those good rules, but to emphasize that other Wiccans needed to listen to their elders and spread their knowledge to later generations. Without accepting the teachings of our elders, the Rede as it is known today may never have formally existed. This would have certainly led to a less widespread message, as word of mouth sometimes leads to disparities in the telling and sharing.

The Wiccan Rede was very quickly adopted and spread by the community as a written poem. This poem's roots may not be commonly known by most, but the words themselves have spread throughout the world. The guidelines set by the Rede are clearly explained and easy to follow.

The Rule of Three

Wiccans are always careful to follow the Rede, actively working to avoid harming others through their actions. Another widely accepted rule in Wicca is known as the rule of three. This is viewed by most as a sort of karmic retribution tied to specific actions. In other words, actions taken by any Wiccan, whether positive or negative, will return to them three times. This is believed to apply to spellwork, acts of charity, or anything else.

Some Wiccans view the rule of three in a near literal interpretation. Giving a dollar to a homeless person will lead to three dollars coming back to you later. Others view it in less stringent terms; for example, offering money to someone in need may lead to a different threefold reward. Maybe instead of directly receiving money back, you will get the job you recently applied for. Maybe your family will be blessed with good health.

As stated above, the rule of three applies to all behaviors, positive or negative, magickal or mundane. Maybe saying something unkind will lead you to spill coffee on your shirt before that job interview. Setting a friend up to fail could result in a fender bender and repair bills. These matters are not always cut and dry, nor are the results always immediate.

All of this, like most analyses of human behavior, is entirely subjective and up to interpretation. With that in mind, the idea of a threefold retribution is usually enough to keep many Wiccans making more positive decisions in their own lives. They do this in the hope that positive actions will be rewarded with more of the same. Though this rule may not be a continual influence over every Wiccan out there, it does what it was intended to do. The rule of three keeps most Wiccans mindful of their actions towards their fellow human beings.

Why This Matters

The Rede and the rule of three form the moral compass for many Wiccans in their everyday lives, and this applies to magical workings as well as mundane life. A Wiccan who is obedient to both these codes is more likely to behave deliberately and positively toward others. They will not throw around magickal curses or impulsive spellwork just to see what happens. Nor would they act spiteful toward a neighbor for no reason. However, these behaviors are not just focused on other people; they also influence the way Wiccans treat themselves.

Wiccans view their own bodies as the most important instrument of any that they might work with. Most will not perform spells while ill out of concern for drawing in negative energies. They strive to only use their magick for good, and to only work magick when properly focused on their desired intent and physically at their best. A Wiccan under the weather may take a step back and pray to deity rather than work a spell. They may also ask another Wiccan friend to work a spell on their behalf instead.

The practice of spellcasting can be controversial to those who know nothing about it. However, as with most things Wicca, the stereotypes don't always match reality. Spellcasting in Wicca can be compared to prayer in other faiths; it is a time set aside for a Wiccan to communicate with their chosen deity or spirits and ask for whatever they desire. Other practices such as crafting spell jars or poppets are considered extra sources of that same hopeful energy, that same effort to fill a need. Of course, as with anything else in our lives, the answer may still end up being no. However, the Rede and the rule of three serves as a moral compass so that Wiccans need not second guess their own desires or the intent behind their spellcraft.

Rumors abound about the existence of 'white magick and black magick', or magick used for purely good or evil purposes. As with most Wiccan stereotypes, these rumors are unfounded. A Wiccan who casts mostly curses, hexes, or charms is not using black magick; they are simply trying to manipulate energies in a way that other Wiccans might not. Magick has no firm moral code. It is simply the manipulation and harnessing of energies in the hopes of creating a desired outcome. There is never any guarantee of anything, even in Wicca.

Chapter 3: Wheel of The Year

Holidays or holy days are common for every religion in the world, and Wicca is no different; Wiccan holidays are marked by a calendar known as the Wheel of the Year. Each of its eight spokes represents holidays commonly known as Sabbats. Wiccan holidays are traditionally celebrated around the full moons, with a Sabbat occurring roughly every six weeks. Many of the holidays are centered around either the changing of the seasons or the harvest; truly, the easiest way to practice Wiccan holy days is to simply pay attention to one's surroundings. The beats of nature are causes for celebration in Wicca. Fertility and abundance are celebrated in spring and summer, and gratitude is expressed for those same blessings later in the year as fall and winter roll in.

There are eight recognized Sabbats in Wicca. Each one has its specific themes, associated deities, and common celebrations. The minor Sabbats mark the beginning for each of the seasons. The major sabbats mark the seasons in the midpoint, at their heights. Don't let the labels of 'major' and 'minor' create preconceived notions of how each holiday is celebrated; each Wiccan holiday can be as simple or as grand in celebration as the person wishes to make it. It is just as easy to have a small ritual to recognize Samhain (the Wiccan new year) as it is to have a large celebration for Yule.

The eight Sabbats are in perfect balance around the wheel of the year. Equinoxes parallel one another, and full moons act as bookends. If you start on the Wiccan new year, the cycle goes full moon, equinox, full moon, equinox, and so on. Each holiday has its role and specific seasonal changes that it recognizes and celebrates. A Wiccan in tune with nature will only rarely miss a Sabbat, even if they don't always celebrate on the correct date.

What matters in Wicca above nearly everything else is *intention*. Offering up recognition to a holy day is better than ignoring it altogether, and there is no real harm in celebrating early or late.

Major Sabbats

Samhain (pronounced sah-win) is the Wiccan new year. It falls on Halloween, traditionally, and the night is thought to be a time that the deceased and other spirits are easier to communicate with. This is the only holiday not specifically tied to a full moon or equinox, though some people may choose to celebrate it on the full moon closest to Halloween. Samhain celebrates the end of the harvest season and marks the start of the year's darkest period, winter. Traditional celebrations for this holiday include leaving food or cakes behind for family members who died over the past year. Modern Wiccans often hold public balls around Samhain to celebrate the previous year.

Imbloc (im-bulk) marks the beginning of spring and is celebrated on February first. It marks the center point of the dark half of the year, and is traditionally associated with Brigid (an Irish goddess) or more generally with the Maiden. As the world prepares for the coming spring, new life is readying itself to emerge. Many Wiccans will create Brigid's Crosses from wheat or corn shucks and exchange them as symbols of prosperity. Spring cleaning is common, eliminating old energies to welcome in new beginnings.

Beltane is also known as May Day, and marks the return of wealth and prosperity to the earth as everything springs to life.

The Sun God's coronation feast is celebrated during this holiday. As the youthful God comes of age, the Goddess does the same and the pair of them are believed to unite. Beltane feasts celebrate their union. Common celebrations include the traditional maypole as well as large gatherings and meals.

Lammas falls in late July or early August; it celebrates the season of fall and the coming harvest. This holiday is associated with ripening grain and a variety of harvest goddesses. Herb harvesting, fresh baked bread, and prosperity spells are common to this season. Gratitude is a common theme and traditional spells include household or hearth magick.

Minor Sabbats

Yule marks the beginning of winter and is traditionally celebrated around Christmastime. This holiday has been heavily adopted by Christians and may be one of the easiest for Wiccans to make mention of publicly. Yule is part of the darkest time of the year, traditionally marked by green boughs being brought inside as well as other reminders that spring will come again.

Ostara is a harvest celebration celebrated during the spring equinox, sometimes referred to as Easter instead. As with Yule, many Ostara celebrations have been adopted by Christianity. Egg hunting is meant to symbolize the harvest and celebrate the fertility of the earth. Flowers start growing and life begins to emerge from the quiet and cold of winter. Ostara celebrations commonly honor a fertility goddess and focus on themes of virility and new life.

Litha falls opposite of Yule on the Wheel. This is a midsummer festival, falling on the longest day of the year when the god is at his greatest strength. Celebrating light and life tend to be big, loud affairs for many Wiccans, but as with most other practices, this is not a requirement. The summer solstice celebrates both the God and Goddess at the height of their powers and capabilities. The harvest is almost ready to be collected and only abundance waits for those who reap.

Mabon is the fall equinox, counterpart to Ostara on the Wheel of the Year. On both these days, the world is in equilibrium with day and night being equal. This celebration is the Wiccan Thanksgiving and a time meant to prepare for the coming winter. The abundance of the harvest is the focus of Mabon, and many Wiccans use this holiday to mark a time of rest after the labor of the harvest. The oak king begins to yield his reign, allowing the holly king to step forward as winter approaches.

Each of these holidays has their traditional place in the calendar year. They all focus primarily on the changing of the seasons and the idea of things being in a specific and logical order. Sowing leads to reaping, winter leads to spring, and even when things seem their darkest, light will always return. Celebrating these changes in the natural world is important to Wiccans as they recognize their own place in nature and their influence on it. As always, the wheel never stops turning.

Chapter 4: Altars

A Wiccan's altar is their workspace and their church in one. It is the place they go to for prayer, offerings, meditation, spellcasting, or other religious rites. An altar can remain static, with the same items in the same places year-round, or it can evolve with new decorations or different tools placed on it for each Sabbat or season. Some Wiccans set up outdoor altars or have a dedicated natural space they like to go to for meditation or spellwork. Others might have a dedicated room in their house. Still, the grandiose is not a requirement for any kind of set-up. An altar can be very tiny and as simple as elemental representations carried in a mint tin.

The altar is very much intended to be a working space. It is not an ornamental area, but something actively used. It should be kept clean, since dust can draw in negative energy. Any pet owners should not be surprised if their four-legged friends are drawn to their altars; this can be particularly common with cats. Some Wiccans believe that it can be a sign of good luck and high positive energy for an animal to be drawn to their altar. Some even encourage this by limiting items on the altar so there is less for a cat to knock down. Altars are also very personal; there is no wrong way to set one up.

All that is needed for an altar is a space that has been blessed. Having a representation of each element (earth, air, water, and fire) can help someone to focus on their spellwork but is not an absolute necessity. These representations can be colors rather than physical objects. A pebble, a feather, a vial of water, and a match all in a small box can be a portable altar. The point of these representations are to act as focus points, things to help the Wiccan in setting their intent for spell work or meditation.

In a pinch, a spell can be cast with entirely empty hands and nothing more than visualizations in the mind.

For those who do intend to work with multiple tools, it is important to be safe about this plan. Do not leave candles or blades unattended. Read up on herbs, plants, fruits, and other ingestible elements before using them in spellwork in order to keep track of what can and cannot be safely ingested. This consideration should apply to any animals that also share space with the altar. If desired, keep an easy to clean surface such as a dropcloth under your altar, as accidents can happen during magickal workings. Fragile items may not be the best choice to be placed on the altar if there are pets or curious children around. Finally, any items you wish to keep private may be better off stored away or in a hidden space rather than kept in the open all the time.

Some people are unable to practice publicly, whether due to other family members or roommates or just a lack of privacy; this is where a mental practice may be the most effective method. Picturing the tools, the candle flames, or anything else tied to spellwork or meditation is a perfectly acceptable method of keeping an altar. A purely mental practice is just as valid as a physical one.

Cardinal Directions

Each of the elements (earth, air, water, and fire) corresponds to one of the four cardinal directions. Traditionally, earth is in the north, air in the east, water in the west, and fire in the south. Some Wiccans may change the specifics, but one element per direction is common enough in every sect. Of course, making these connections means a person needs to know where their cardinal directions are. This is not as difficult as it might seem.

The easiest two directions to identify are east and west. The sun rises in the east and sets in the west. If you stand facing the east, north will be to your right and south to your left. If you stand facing the west, north will be to your left and south to your right. Remembering these directions can help with altar setup, especially if you have a larger setup such as a dedicated room. The fifth element, spirit, is represented in the center of the cast circle as well as all around. These elements are tied to each point in the pentagram, a popular Wiccan symbol depicted as a star with a circle around it.

Connecting the elements to cardinal directions is the easiest part of the process for altar setup. Moving beyond that to spellwork can make things more complicated. From colors to symbols to animals, each of the cardinal directions can be tied to many other symbols. Wiccans like to use these different relationships to add a sort of boost to their spellwork. It is believed that a bounty of correct correspondences can be included in a spell as a show of understanding and respect to the deities and energies involved.

Correspondences

Correspondences are a sort of representation or symbolism for each of the elements and their cardinal directions. They act as focus points to help a Wiccan pay full attention to the intent of their spellwork, whatever the desired outcome may be. Focus points prevent distraction or a waning focus and help Wiccans to better understand and recall the aims and goals of their spells. The color green, for example, might feature heavily in an abundance spell. These correspondences can be specific colors, animals, plants, or other symbols that represent each element or direction.

Earth is the element commonly tied to the north. It draws on feminine energy and represents strength, abundance, wealth, and stability. Practicing herbalism and knot magick are common ways to honor the element. Ways to include earth more in practice include gardening, burying items underground, and crafting items out of wood or stone. When burying things, make sure that nothing going into the ground is toxic or incapable of breaking down.

Air is the element tied to the east. It channels masculine energy and represents dreams and wishes, psychic powers, inspiration, communication, and the mind. Breeze, feathers, and breath are some of the common symbols for this element. The spider, eagle, and raven are three animals associated with the air. Lighting incense and watching the smoke can be a straightforward meditation and a way to honor the spirits of the east. Common spellwork that would focus on air as a primary element include soul seeking, counteracting negative thoughts, and karma work.

Fire is connected to the south. This destructive element must be treated with extreme respect and caution. Many Wiccans choose to only work directly with fire when they are outside to allow for better control over it; it is also good practice to never leave a candle burning unattended. Fire is the element of change, associated with anger, passion, and the heat of the day. Fire-centered spells include things like walking away from relationships, love spells, and spells to give someone more emotional strength. Red, crimson, orange, and white are some of the associated colors. Fire is common in any kind of candle magick.

Water is the element connected to the west. This ever-shifting element is symbolized by the color blue. Water has feminine energy and seems capable of getting through anything with enough time and patience. It represents wisdom, emotions, and the subconscious. Water-centered spells include healing spells, brew making, and ritual bathing. Turquoise, black, indigo, and green are some of the colors that represent this element.

Using these correspondences, just as nearly everything else in Wicca, is not a hard and fast rule. It is just another tool to help focus energies and drive motivation. Having the perfect colored candles or the correct moon phase can help quite a lot, but these things are not an absolute necessity every time. For beginners, however, it can be better to try following the correspondences as closely as possible. Cast banishing spells during a new moon. Draw in positive energy or blessings during a full moon. Gather strength or courage during a waxing moon. Draw in peace and cast out negativity during a waning moon. Once you've mastered your focus by utilizing correspondences correctly, you may find that your spellwork comes easier with fewer correspondences in a pinch.

Chapter 5: Working Tools

Tools are not a necessity in Wicca; a person can practice Wicca or cast spells with no more accessories than their own body. A knife (normally called an athame) or wand may be two of the most common tools seen on a Wiccan's altar. Statues to represent deities and small items to represent each element are also present. Other possible tools include candles of various colors (though a white candle can be used for any spell), divination tools such as a pendulum or tarot card deck, small bottles or jars for crafting spells, various herbs, and much more. Wicca can involve a great number of props, if desired, but it is important to remember that they are not absolutely necessary.

All of these tools are usually personal to the Wiccan who owns them. One person's wand may be a plain stick. Another might have a well-crafted and varnished piece of wood that they whittled, shaped, and sanded themselves. Both are equally valid. Any Wiccan is also allowed to acquire any of their tools themselves if they wish. There is zero truth to the idea, for example, that a person's first tarot deck must be gifted to them (though some do adhere to this practice merely out of tradition). Likewise, wands do not have to be gifted or even handmade.

The wand or athame are commonly used to direct the flow of energy, essentially acting as an extension of the Wiccan's hand or fingers. The athame can also be used for cutting things for or during a ritual, such as harvesting herbs or crafting working tools if necessary. This is a matter of personal taste and safety. Some Wiccans keep their athame as merely symbolic and do not sharpen it. The athame and the wand are the most commonly used pair of tools on any Wiccan's altar; however, most Wiccans, even if they choose to work without tools, will at least acquire a wand.

Divination tools may be some of the most controversial. Some Wiccans cast runes or use a pendulum for their divination. Others will meditate on shapes in smoke or study the clouds. Still others use their tarot decks. Most divination is not the exact science that some might make it out to be. After all, not everyone is meant to know everything. Despite this, there are some Wiccans who give a lot of focus to divination through tools such as the tarot.

The tarot deck consists of seventy-eight cards with twenty-two in the major arcana and the remaining fifty-six in the minor arcana. The major arcana has specifically named cards (the fool, the lovers, justice, etc.), and each card has its own meanings, interpretations, and symbols. The minor arcana consists of suits: pentacles, swords, wands, and cups. The meaning of each card depends on its position when it is laid down. A positive interpretation is usually assigned if the card is upright; a negative interpretation is more likely should the card be reversed or upside down. These meanings are also widely varied. The tower, for example, is almost universally viewed as a bad card, a sign of trials and tribulations. However, it does not always mean that sheer destruction is coming or that the person the card applies to will not make it through whatever comes.

A chalice is used to hold liquid offerings for the divine, salt water to be blessed, or small libations for ceremony. This can be a simple cup or something fancier. Some people use special jeweled cups, but it can be as basic as a coffee cup. Other symbolic tools in Wicca include a libation dish used for non-liquid offerings. After these offerings have been presented on the altar for the deity, they can be poured or buried in the earth or into a moving body of water to be carried to the divine.

Candles are very popular items on altars and are commonly used to represent the deities being worshipped. They can also be used in spellwork, with different colors tied to different meanings. Green for wealth, gold for spirit, red for romance, and so on. These correspondences are not set in stone, and it is usually better practice to follow intuition when choosing supplies for a spell or for an altar setup. When in doubt, white candles can replace any other color.

This is just a small sampling of the tools that can be placed on an altar. Some people use special altar cloths to cover the work surface and/or to cover offerings or libations. Mirrors can be used for banishing spells to reflect negativity back to whomever sent it out. Flowers or local plants can be used as decoration or as further offerings. There is an abundance of options here for Wiccans to consider; just remember that none of this is necessary, but they can be enjoyable to collect and select for different purposes and can improve spell efficacy when used correctly.

Creating Versus Buying

Gathering tools is entirely a matter of taste. Some people like to craft their own working tools for Wicca, such as carving a wand or planting their own herb garden. Others prefer to buy. Even when buying tools, there are different schools of thought as to how to go about it. Some people will buy items such as small jars or vials in bulk or from a big box store. Other people prefer something that has a personal touch to it— for example, buying something handmade that they might not have the skill or time to craft themselves such as an altar cloth. There is no true difference between these ideals, and a spell cast by handcrafted items can have the same energy as manufactured items.

Handcrafted items can feel nicer and contain more personal energy upfront from the crafting process, especially when crafted by the caster. That being said, even a store-bought item will eventually begin to pick up its owner's energies. As long as a Wiccan has the ability to focus their mind, they can cast a spell using nothing more than their own body. Try mentally picturing a candle flame or pointing a finger to cast a circle. It works, but may be hard to visualize for beginners; tools are just there to make the job a little easier.

Whether buying or crafting tools, it may be best to start small. A wand (which can be as simple as a stick one feels drawn to) and two candles to represent the deities would be an excellent start for someone new to Wicca. Nobody needs to go out and build a full altar for their very first spell. Instead, work small and slow to see what works and build from there. Some Wiccans practice exclusively in their kitchen (and are called kitchen witches) and use their magick by adding positive energy and love into food as they prepare it. Others may practice exclusively outdoors, only using the tools that nature provides. There is no one way to practice, nor is there just one way to find the right tools.

Using temporary tools while waiting for the perfect one is also completely acceptable. If crafting a wand is on the to-do list but only the stick has been obtained so far, use the soon-to-be carved stick or a finger in the interim. Use a favorite coffee mug as a chalice in one ritual, then wash it and use it the next morning for your daily caffeine fix. There are no hard-and-fast rules that items are required to be set aside specifically for ritual at all times, though it is recommended. This recommendation is based more on establishing a special space than it is on any kind of requirement. You can cast a last-minute spell with a stick found on the ground, a handful of dirt, and a bottle of water, but it will generally be more effective to use dedicated items and a dedicated space for spellwork, especially for people new to Wicca.

Dried herbs versus fresh herbs is another common debate among Wiccans. Some people enjoy having a personal herb garden for spellwork as well as for food and healing. Others may not have the time or the space and prefer a spice rack to digging in the ground. This, as with much else, is entirely a matter of preference. Fresh herbs generally provide no better results in spellwork than dried.

One practice that modern-day Wiccans generally agree is to be avoided is the use of live animals or animal parts in spellwork. Anyone who might decide to do so are careful about what parts they use, gather, or share. An animal that died of natural causes with their remains gathered and cleaned in a respectful manner might make an appearance on a Wiccan's altar if they have an affinity with that creature. This usually comes in the form of small bones or bits of fur. Nevertheless, this tends to be the exception rather than the rule. For most Wiccans, the most you might find on their altar are bird feathers. Even then, some prefer to use artificial feathers that have been dyed to match realistic ones as there is no way to guarantee how the feather in question was lost.

Let Them Come to You

One of the most effective ways to find the right tool is, ironically, to stop looking for it. Sometimes the right tool will find its way to you. A random empty book on a shelf might become your book of shadows. A rock that feels right in your hand may be your representation of earth. A found item that comes out of nowhere may end up being one of your most used and cherished tools.

Do remember that these accessories are not necessary and that if a tool no longer serves a purpose, it does not need to stay on your altar. Try not to keep something on an altar just because it has sentimental value. If it's special enough to warrant keeping, find another place for it. It might even end up serving a mundane purpose, if that feels right. If it is not serving a purpose on an altar other than taking up space, it does not need to be there.

Tools in Wicca are generally meant to be used. The only exception might be elemental representations or deity statues, but even those items are not meant to be static. They should be touched, recognized, and treated as more than mere ornamentation. No matter which tools end up on the altar, don't let them gather dust. That can draw in more negative energy and make spellcasting more difficult in terms of getting a specific outcome.

Though gathering tools can be entertaining and can even teach a Wiccan more about themselves, remember again that they are not necessary. You do not need a wand or candles or a chalice or anything else in order to practice Wicca. These working tools are meant to add to your focus and allow you to perform better, more accurate spellwork. Having tools can offer a more specialized outcome, such as an abundance spell resulting in a raise at work rather than merely finding a five-dollar bill on the street.

When it comes to collecting tools, working deliberately will lead to the best outcome and can reward you with tools you can use for many years. Whether handcrafted or store-bought or even intangible, tools can increase your understanding and skill when it comes to casting spells, meditating, or just being mindful of your actions. Just as your altar is meant to be a working space, holy without being set apart, so too are your tools meant to be used. Something ornamental or fragile may not stand up well to constant use. Better to have something you can imprint with your personal energy.

Chapter 6: Putting It Together

With deities selected, an altar set up, and tools in hand, the real work of Wicca can begin. This faith does not involve paying lip service to deities or attending scheduled worship in special buildings. Instead, Wiccans can cast spells or pray at any time. Deities and the elements are always there to listen and help in any way they can. Wiccans need no special space or specific words unless a script is desired for actions such as blessing items, cleansing items, or crafting. Even then, following intuition can be a fine guide with no specific words required. The behavior of casting spells can be more complicated and require deliberation. Wiccans have to work for it and will only get out of their religious practice what they put into it.

Spellcasting is one of the most intricate practices in Wicca. It commonly involves casting a circle by calling the quarters, which is followed by asking the deities or spirit to witness the act, protect the caster, and to intercede on the caster's behalf. Spells can be cast for many different purposes including protection, banishment, good luck, and much more. In addition to casting spells, some Wiccans choose to craft items like good luck charms or altar decorations for additional blessings. These items can be imbued with energy for specific purposes, such as banishing negative thoughts.

Meditation is another common practice among Wiccans. This can be more difficult to learn and get comfortable with, especially for those who have never tried it. Put simply, meditation involves quieting the mind and drawing the focus toward the breath. This can help relax the body, ground a person in the current moment and location, and give the subconscious mind time to work through problems similar to the way it does in dreams. Random or intrusive thoughts are expected, especially when someone is new to the practice. With time, however, a person can learn to recognize these random thoughts and let them pass by rather than dwelling on them or analyzing them. Focusing on the breath shifts the mental state over time to one of greater relaxation and awareness.

As your body begins to drift and your thoughts cycle, you can keep focusing on your breathing until you are ready to slowly return to your day. A good meditation session can leave people energized afterward with their minds relaxed; they feel calm and at peace.

All in all, the most important practice among Wiccans is probably mindfulness. This is another action that requires practice to get right. Mindfulness is the act of behaving with deliberation; it involves living in the moment rather than dwelling on future possibilities or past pain. Many people find this difficult to do because it is so unusual in our busy and interconnected modern society. People are subject to so much new information and stress on a daily basis that it can prevent them from focusing on the present moment, let alone the world around them.

Behaving with mindfulness can help a person to be more aware of their actions. Someone who is mindful will understand more about their surroundings as well. They might know ahead of time that a friend is upset, picking up on micro-expressions that others would not see. Likewise, someone who is mindful will pay more attention to how other people react to them, and they can adjust behaviors accordingly to get a better outcome from personal interactions.

Treating others with care is something all Wiccans try to do. They do not behave rashly or hastily and work to keep their lives in balance. This extends beyond fellow humans and applies to nature as well. Treating every living thing with respect is likely to lead to better spellcasting, increased understanding of spell correspondences, and a higher chance of gaining the desired outcome, perhaps even in a shorter timeline. Additionally, treating living creatures with respect can return the same behavior to you in a great karmic cycle that improves the lives of everyone.

Keep It Simple

Some of the basics of Wicca can be overwhelming, and there is so much for beginners to learn. Elements, correspondences, moon phases, symbolic colors, rhymes, and all the other considerations to making everything perfect can make the act of spellcasting seem impossible. Full moons are for the strongest spellwork, waxing moons for drawing things in, waning moons for blocking things out, and on top of all that there are specific days of the week that are better suited to some spells than others. The more details a person goes looking for in Wicca, the more they will find.

What matters in spellcasting is intention. If you cast a spell trying to bless your household or help with a job search or anything else positive, it is likely that the energy you send out will add to your efforts and ultimately yield good results. Cast your spells with the desire to do good. That will help you more than studying the minute the moon is at its fullest or trying to find a candle in the perfect shade of red.

Intention also makes a difference when it comes to hexes or curses. Casting a spell against someone should be even more carefully considered than other spellwork. Even Wiccans cannot take away another person's free will. When someone acts against you, it may be more helpful to solve the root of the problem rather than strike back. If, however, a curse or hex becomes the only solution, you need to know how to protect yourself.

When performing a spell against someone else, it is important that you keep yourself protected as well. Consider the rule of three and the Rede. Add a reflective shield to prevent the person you are working against from retaliating. Most importantly, do not take such a harsh action lightly at all. Be entirely sure before you reach for spellwork of any kind to fix your problems.

All the tools, correspondences, moon phases, and the rest only become as complex and important as you make it. For beginners it might be easier just to send out good energy and wait for it to come back or bear fruit. Take an active role in your spiritual life, but do not get so bogged down in minutiae that you forget the mundane. It is always more important to try to find a mundane solution to a problem than it is to jump to a magickal one.

The act of spellcasting is akin to taking a more active role in your own religious life rather than sitting back and waiting for prayers to be answered. As the saying goes, the gods help those who help themselves. Casting a spell can be compared to the idea of meeting a deity halfway, as if a person is fulfilling their part of a deal so that the deity will finish the rest. This allows Wiccans to put effort into getting the outcome they desire without having full control or astounding power as some stereotypes would have people believe. If Wiccans knew any better than the rest of us what the future held, it's likely that knowledge would make them miserable. Nobody should know everything that's coming all the time, and Wiccans are no exception.

So much in Wicca depends on interpretation, knowledge, and practice. Everything in these practices is affected by change, and it is all meant to evolve. From the tools on an altar to the spells used in practice, everything in Wicca is meant to be just as fluid as the cycle of nature around us. Nothing in nature lasts forever without changing in some form, and Wiccan practices are exactly the same. A Wiccan is meant to change and evolve with their faith as they grow.

There are a variety of Wiccan traditions, from the Gardnerian practices discussed earlier to the Hellenic (wherein practitioners worship ancient Greek deities) and so many more. Each of these traditions has minor differences, but all look the same when you get down to the basics. They are polytheistic, they honor nature, and they depend on their practitioners to behave like decent human beings. These commonalities can be found across many traditions, covens, and practices. All the rest, from casting spells to setting up an altar, are nothing more than alternate ways to connect to deities, to the world, and to the self.

Undoing A Spell

One extremely important thing for every Wiccan to know is how to undo a spell. This is not an easy thing to do; it requires work, but is entirely possible. The first thing to be aware of is knowing exactly what type of spell you are looking to undo. A spell you cast will require different actions to reverse than a spell cast against you. One of the easiest methods to reverse any negative act against you is to simply cleanse and shield.

This is a very simple process that starts with a bath. Physical cleanliness is a first important step which comes before spiritual cleanliness. You can add oils to the water if you wish, or cast a small blessing beforehand. Relax in the water and feel your body slowly becoming clean. Scrub everything, though be sure to wash your hair before adding oils to the water. After you are clean, take a moment to meditate. Place your feet against the ground and imagine roots flowing all the way down to the earth's core. Breathe deep, envisioning white healing energy flowing into you with each inhale. Let your body fill up with it. Then send that energy out, crafting a shield around your own body. You can place that shield close to your body or further away, whatever makes you feel comfortable.

This shield can be altered as needed. You can add positive energy to it and make it more solid or more malleable. You can craft it to allow some things to pass through and others to be blocked out. This shield can be made to block negativity and can even be mended throughout the day with the same meditative act as described above. Simply ground, center, and picture the shield again. Add more energy from the earth and rebuild as needed.

Another important method in trying to reverse spellwork is the practice of destroying spell components. This should only be done to components that are single-use and can be easily replaced. Herbs can be buried or burned, wax from candles can be melted and buried, and incense ashes can be scattered to the wind. Other spell components such as mirrors, dishes, and more expensive tools which are meant to be used more than once can be cleansed of the previous spell's energies and made new for other spellwork.

When undoing a spell that you have cast, one of the easier methods involves a candle, water, and a black bowl. Light the candle and let some wax melt to stick the candle to the bottom of the bowl. Once it is standing on its own, add water to the bowl. As the candle burns, state the following:

This spell I do not need.

From its work I will be freed.

Thank you for the work you did.

Now, release, as I have bid.

Picture the bonds of the spell dissolving, severing, or burning, whichever you prefer. Then let the candle burn down until it hits the water and the flame goes out on its own. Once finished, bury the remaining wax and pour the water onto the ground or into a body of running water.

Another method that can be used to undo your own spellcasting is to simply reverse the entire process of casting it. This can be difficult if you do not remember all details of the spell you are trying to reverse. If you are not documenting all of your spellcasting, you could try and follow intuition to reverse the original working or use the method described above instead.

Undoing a spell someone else has cast can be difficult, even impossible, unless you know specifics of what they did. If a curse or hex was cast against you, it is probable that the caster also built in protective fail-safes for themselves. This means that reflecting the curse back at them or anything similar is unlikely to work. In this case the best thing to do is simply shield yourself rather than try to strike back. If you can, talk to the person who worked the spell and see if they would consider reversing it themselves. This is a prime example of seeking mundane solutions first, which is very important in Wicca.

Though spellwork can be fulfilling, fascinating, and even entertaining, it should never be the first answer a Wiccan reaches for with every problem. It is always better to send out good energy than bad and better still to deal with matters in a mundane fashion before looking at spellwork. Nevertheless, if a spell is needed, the sky's the limit in terms of what you can do to help achieve a particular desired outcome.

Chapter 7: Spells and Rituals

The first thing a beginner Wiccan must know how to do is cast a circle. The magickal circle acts as a barrier between the worlds of the magickal and the mundane. It is erected to keep the caster and any other believers within safe from negative energies or malicious spirits. It also acts as a special marker, similar to the way other faiths seek out a specific building for their worship. Wiccans need no such special building, so casting a circle marks the spot as temporarily holy or blessed. It also serves as protection from all sides, ensuring that no negative energy or malicious spirits can cause trouble. The circle is in fact more like a dome, protecting above, below, and all around.

Casting a circle is serious business, and a Wiccan who does so would do well to make sure everything they need for their spellwork or worship is inside the circle before it is cast. This is because the act of crossing in and out without dismantling what has been built first breaks down the magickal energies within the circle. This breakdown can lead to a weaker spell among other repercussions. If a circle must be crossed during ritual work, this can be done by cutting a door– usually a single cut, similar to how a tent flap might be made.

The first step in casting a circle is to call the quarters. This act is done in each quadrant, with guardians or elemental energies sometimes called upon to act as protectors while the circle is up. Some Pagans begin this process in the north with the element of earth. After that, they go east to honor the element of air, south for fire, and west for water. Once all four quadrants have been called, the Wiccan will stand in the center of the circle and invite their chosen god and goddess to view their rites. This action is done as a gesture of welcoming, inviting the deity and the representative spirits of each element to witness the magickal rite about to be requested. Now the circle is cast and spellwork can commence.

What the spellwork *is* hardly matters to the process of creating and bringing down the circle. A spell casting can last as long as it needs to; the only time limit is one you set for yourself. Blessings, charms, or hexes can all be cast safely within the circle. Any casting that is done without a magickal circle can be more dangerous as there is no spiritual protection for the caster. Still, some Wiccans will choose to do small workings without a circle first. This is all a matter of preference.

Taking down a circle is done in the reverse. The god and/or goddess are thanked for their presence first and invited to leave or stay, as they wish. Beginning in the west and ending in the north, any guardians, deities, or elements that may have chosen to join are politely dismissed. There is usually a variation given for each that can be summed up as 'go if you must, but stay if you like'. This phrasing is important because Wiccans do not casually boss around any sort of magickal creature or deity. They chose to join and so can choose to depart on their own timeline, whatever that may be.

Casting a circle can be done bare-handed, with only one pointing finger indicating where the circle is. Some Wiccans choose to use their wand or athame instead. Whatever tool was used to cast the circle should be used again to take it down. Leaving a circle up can cause the energies that created it to slowly deteriorate; this can change the energy or even the intent of whatever spell might have been cast within the circle. Beginners may want to physically mark the boundaries of their circle to keep family members or housemates from crossing through the magickal barrier. Pets and small children are usually considered immune: if they pass through unknowingly, there should be no negative effect on the spell being worked.

Four Basic Spells

Spells can be cast for any reason or intent that can be imagined. This chapter will lay out four straightforward spells: one to draw in prosperity, two to banish negative energy, and one to bless items. These building block spells are easy to understand and perform. They can be used, changed, or adapted to fit nearly any need. The words provided can be replaced with different ones if the intent is not quite right for your needs. Items can be blessed to attract wealth, health, or positive energy. Banishing can put up shields against negative energy, harsh words, or bad moods. Drawing in positive energy can potentially result in prosperity, friendship, or love.

An important thing to remember is that no spellwork should ever be performed without deep thought and deliberation ahead of time. Wicca is not a cure-all for life's problems and does not grant what might commonly be known as magic powers. Spellwork should be done in the safety of a magick circle whenever possible. Some small works of magick may not need it, such as tossing invisible balls of positive energy into a room of fighting children. For beginners in Wicca, however, it is better to stick with the basics and give yourself time to grow in your craft.

Practitioners of Wicca often find that their skills and spells change over their time in the faith as they become more experienced. Some Wiccans are better at specific spells or charms than others. Improvement comes with time, and practicing only one type of spell can inadvertently lead others to weaken due to neglect. Spells also can and should change over time to become more effective or to achieve specific results. For example, blessing an item may seem a similar spell as one which sets it up to deflect negative energy, but these are in fact very different approaches to the same problem.

This kind of flexibility is important in spellwork. It can help Wiccans to find multiple solutions and keep them from using one spell over and over, especially if it does not lead to an intended result. Beginners should track all of their spells with as much detail as possible, from the time of the day the spell was completed to the words that were said. This not only makes a spell easier to undo, but also offers more education into what works and what doesn't and makes it easier for other spells to be adjusted for greater effectiveness.

Prosperity Spell

Remember that all tools can be visualized rather than physical, but if desired, you may gather your wand or athame, a green candle, some water, and salt. After casting a circle, mix together the salt and water using your finger, wand, or athame. Then, ask a deity to bless the salt water. Use the water to anoint the candle, working from the top down and avoiding the wick. As you light the candle, say these words:

Candle flame, burning strong.

I ask for blessings ere too long.

Let good things be drawn to me;

as I ask, so mote it be.

You may repeat these words as often as you think feels right. After that, sit quietly and watch the flame for a few minutes. Use this time to visualize what you want drawn to you. It could be wealth or good luck or friendship. Once you are finished, thank the deity and the elemental energies for assisting you and for hearing your request. Allow the candle to burn down if it is safe to do so. Bury the remaining candle or resulting ball of wax.

Banishing Spell

A banishing spell is intended to block out negativity. Tools you may add if desired include water, a ziplock bag, small pieces of paper, and a writing tool. On the paper, write some of the things you no longer want in your life. Think about these seriously and be honest with yourself. Maybe you need to gossip less or maybe a co-worker needs less direct support from you for their problems. Take the paper you've written on, put it in the bag, and add water. Bring the bag into your circle once it is properly sealed. Envision what life will look like without these negative influences and behaviors as you say the following:

Let these all stop

frozen in ice.

Let me be better

and help me be nice.

Repeat the words as many times as you think feels right, passing the sealed bag from hand to hand. When you are ready, bring down your circle and put the bag in the freezer. Once it is completely frozen you may dispose of it in the trash, through burying, or by putting the whole thing (except the zip lock bag) into a moving body of water.

Another banishing spell can be cast using a piece of paper, black salt, a bowl, and a mirror. This spell is intended to be used against a person who may be causing trouble in your life. Write their name on the paper, place it in the bowl, and cover it in black salt. Then, state the following while imagining the person's negativity bouncing back at them:

I end this hurt by deflecting you.

All you say, no longer true.

Your harm will strike no longer.

Reflect back at you stronger.

After you have said the words a sufficient amount, bury the paper and salt and cleanse the bowl and mirror (physically as well as magickally via a blessing) for later use. The reusing of items is common in Wicca and can safely be done as long as the items are cleaned between uses.

Blessing Items

Items for this spell if desired include salt, water, any color candle, a feather, and the items to be blessed. This can include your entire altar if desired. Cast the circle, inviting elemental representatives and a deity to join and witness the work. After that, the items to be blessed will be laid out on the altar. Each item in turn will have the salt and water sprinkled over them, the lit candle passed over them, and each item will be touched with the feather. This assures that each item has been blessed by the four elements. After that, ask the deity to do the same. Meditate. Pray, if you prefer that word. Ask for the blessings you need.

Are these items being blessed to be your working tools on your altar? Are they being blessed to draw prosperity or good luck to you? Are you making a love charm or other specific trinket? Be honest about your intent and remember that you can only control your own actions and not the actions of others. You can ask, for example, to show some of the traits you have that a crush might like seeing in a partner. You cannot ask for someone to fall in love with you, as you have no control over them.

After you have made your request, meditate a while before taking down your circle. If possible, leave the items out overnight to be blessed by the moon's energy as well. Placing them outdoors or near a window would be better, but this is not a necessity if you don't have the means.

Crafting Items

This is not always common for every Wiccan, but can be very fulfilling to those who choose to go this route. The practice of item crafting can include a variety of practices from woodwork or sewing to making spell jars or cooking food. Spell jars are a combination of herbs, stones, and other correspondences all gathered for a specific purpose. They are usually blessed with a set intention and can be carried around or placed in a special location, such as a blessing jar designed to draw in well-wishing visitors placed outside the entrance to a home.

Spellwork and positive energy in general can be added to anything; they can be a part of any crafting, magickal or mundane. All that is required is knowledge of the craft and knowledge of the spellwork or energy one wishes to add or manipulate. Woodwork can be used to craft good luck charms or figures to be burned as part of a spell. Even a meal can be imbued with positive energy or healing.

There is a wide variety of practices that can combine crafting and Wicca. It can even be possible to combine these without being crafty if you bless the raw materials ahead of time and pass them on to someone else. All forms of crafting items are time-consuming, so this process is not made for hasty spellwork. However, this practice does keep to the ideals of Wicca. If you take time to cook a meal or carve a charm, you will have plenty of time to focus on what you want to imbue it with. The effort to create it will add to the effort of casting the spell, resulting in a more potent outcome.

Spellwork 101

There are many different types of spells out there, but two spell types that don't exist in Wicca are the concepts of 'white magick' and 'black magick'. Those terms are a polarized view of spellwork, identifying individual spells as good or bad based on intent. Intent, however, is the key to answering the entire question. No spellwork is truly bad unless the caster is being genuinely malicious against their target. A person with ill intent might try to curse a gossiper with a bad case of laryngitis to shut them up. This would be a very dangerous and negative spell to perform. On the other hand, a person with good intent might cast a spell to grant themselves patience and then take mundane steps to avoid being stuck in a conversation with the gossiper, such as avoiding their desk at work. In this case, the caster has good intent and has taken non-magickal steps to solve the problem at hand, likely resulting in good energy and a positive outcome returning to them threefold.

Even in spellwork you can only change yourself, your actions, and your reactions. There are plenty of spells that can be cast against people who may wish you ill, and they are certainly out there for people to find. One example involves stopping nasty rumors by wrapping the mouth of a small doll or poppet shut and then freezing or burning it. However, the possible downside with casting spells specifically to take action against other people is that we never know the full story. The workplace gossip mentioned earlier might have no outlet at home and need that time for socializing. Regardless of intention, it is better not to depend on taking away another person's agency when the time comes to decide which spells to cast. There is no guarantee that such a request will be fulfilled.

Even if the request is fulfilled, the rule of three clearly states that any spellwork designed to take away someone else's agency would not end well for the caster. Most Wiccans don't even share when they cast a small spell, believing that keeping such things more secretive will make the request more likely to be answered. Larger spells (perhaps cast by a coven or performed outdoors) can certainly look impressive, but the reality is that a spell needs no more complexity than a prayer. *Lord and Lady, please bless me with more prosperity, generosity, willingness to help others,* etc. It's that simple, and that is all it ever has to be.

The props and extras can be interesting and different, but often serve as similar ornamentation to the robes a priest might wear. Using tools and casting a circle automatically sets that time and space aside as different, that ground as temporarily holy. Aside from these actions which are used to separate the magickal from the mundane, it is important to remember that the simplest solution is often the best. Spellwork is not meant to be a cure-all for life's every problem.

That being said, this practice can be wonderfully beneficial to the individual. It can open a person up to new communities, possibilities, and knowledge in addition to revealing new connections and capabilities. Wicca is a religion with few rules, good core values, multiple interpretations, and a wonderful feeling of wholeness and balance. Though it is different from many of the other faiths people are used to and comfortable with, Wicca can be fulfilling for anyone.

Conclusion

As this book has hopefully shown, the Wiccan faith is not what most people believe it to be. The majority of the stereotypes surrounding this faith are entirely incorrect and are the result of little more than fear mongering and a lack of education. These beliefs are as varied as their practitioners, and covens and solitary practitioners can be found all over the world. People who practice Wicca seldom wish others ill or throw around curses unless they have fully considered the act and all possible ramifications. Bragging about amazing power or the ability to manipulate energies is the mark of a novice.

There are as many ways to practice Wicca as there are Wiccans in the world. Meditation, spellcasting, and simple mindfulness are all legitimate ways to practice. Likewise, a daily walk in nature can be just as spiritually fulfilling as a diet change or a dedicated altar. Pacifism, vegetarianism, and other lifestyle choices are entirely optional. Most Wiccans choose to take on their problems on a case-by-case basis and will not tie every bad thing in their life solely to their faith or magickal workings.

Everything in Wicca only needs to be as complicated or as simple as one person chooses to make them. Someone who works better with others might seek out a coven to work with. Those who prefer to work alone are free to do so with no problems. A Wiccan may practice alone for their entire lives or may only seek out the company of fellow Wiccans during Sabbats. The same goes for working with deities; it's a matter of choice.

Everything in Wicca may seem to be flexible to the point of having no base, but that is one of the greatest advantages to this faith. The roots it does have are minimal, but they go quite deep.

From Gerald Gardner to Scott Cunningham to modern Wiccans casting their circles and celebrating their Sabbats, they all revere nature and its cycle. They all work hard to treat others well and keep themselves at their best. They keep to the Rede and the rule of three and above all they try to keep on learning.

All that any of us can do is better ourselves and improve from the previous day. This is a process that will look different for everyone. One person may spend less money; another will devote more time to family. Whatever small measure of success you can apply to your life, Wicca and mindfulness can multiply that with dedication and hard work. This faith encourages self-awareness and self-improvement. More than anything, it is welcoming of all.

This book is meant for new Wiccans and anyone who is curious to know what it's all about. If you have chosen this work as your starting point in learning about Wicca, I thank you for your time. Go forward in love and light. Add more beauty to the world. Blessed be!

A Self-Initiation

The following ceremony has been included for new Wiccans who wish to dedicate themselves to the craft. This ceremony is meant to be serious, personal, and private. It can be performed by any person who is willing to follow the tenets, open themselves up to new experiences, and explore a diverse faith. All that is needed is a small drink, a cake or bread, and your own body. A ritual bath prior to performing this ritual is preferred, but not required. You should have an idea of which deities or spirits you will be inviting in and worshipping.

To start, call the elements and cast the circle, beginning in the north. You may use whatever words spring to mind, or state the following:

Guardians of the (direction), ambassadors of (element),

Please witness this magickal work and bless it.

Protect me as I do this work and let it enrich my life.

Thank you for your presence.

After you have called the quarters, address the goddess and god of your choice in the same way. Invite them to witness your dedication. Then, move on to the act itself:

I hereby announce to the universe my intention to worship and revere the goddess (name) and the god (name). I hope that I am able to honor them and follow them with good grace and a kind heart. Let my actions please them as much as possible and demonstrate their acceptance.

If you wish to say more, do so now. These words can be entirely private between you and the deity. You can make more vows or choose a private name for yourself to be used only when you are at your altar or casting a spell. This name can be found by casting runes, finding aspects of nature that resonate with you, following your intuition, or any number of other methods. A new name is not necessary, but can be helpful to new Wiccans to set their faith and its practices aside as special and different.

Meditate for a few moments if you like, perhaps burning a candle or incense. Then take a drink from your offering cup, feeling it flow into your body while you consider the connection your drink has to nature. Water from springs, juice from fruits, and even sodas from sugarcane can all apply to this process. Everything came from nature in one way or another. Repeat the process with your bread or cake. Make sure to leave some of the food and drink behind to act as an offering to the earth or spirit.

Once you have finished and feel the work is completed, you may dismiss the deities, then each of the quarters in the reverse order that you called them:

Hail (deity or elemental quarter), I thank you for your presence.

I thank you for your protection and blessings.

Go if you must; stay if you like.

(After dismissing the final elemental quadrant)

The circle is open but never broken. So mote it be.

With that, it is done. Make your offerings and get rid of any incense or candle remains. You have initiated yourself as a Wiccan. Welcome to the circle.

www.ingramcontent.com/pod-product-compliance
Lightning Source LLC
LaVergne TN
LVHW021737060526
838200LV00052B/3333